LEARNING TOGETHER

Sequential Repertoire for Solo Strings or String Ensemble

By Winifred Crock, William Dick, and Laurie Scott

Performers on the CD:
Kiyoshi Tamagawa, *piano*
Winifred Crock, *violin*
Laurie Scott, *violin*
William Dick, *viola*
Nathan Ledgerwood, *cello*
Melissa Kraut, *solo cello*
Jesus Villareal, *solo bass*

SUMMY-BIRCHARD INC.

© 2010 Summy-Birchard Music
division of Summy-Birchard, Inc.
Exclusive print rights administered by Alfred Music
All rights reserved

ISBN-10: 0-7390-6833-4
ISBN-13: 978-0-7390-6833-5

Contents

We would like to acknowledge the indispensable help of
Dr. Kiyoshi Tamagawa
in the completion and editing of the piano parts.

Introduction

This volume and compact disk contain a sequential unison repertoire for all orchestral stringed instruments. This solo repertoire develops the technique of each player with a uniform strategy for all instruments and facilitates unison playing while the harmony and bass parts provide ensemble possibilities.

The following concepts are important to a successful learning process.

Students should:

- Listen to the enclosed CD every day.
- Learn the repertoire first by ear through repetitive listening and rote preview, not by reading the music notation.
- Play, practice and perform the repertoire from memory.
- Review and polish repertoire during every practice to develop tone, technical ease and musicality.

Teachers should:

- Encourage and develop parent education and involvement in their students' music education and practice.

How to Use The CD

The enclosed CD is the most important part of this purchase. As music repertoire is more easily learned through repetitive daily listening, students learning this music should listen to the CD several times each day. In addition students should listen to the CD many times before beginning to play each piece. Optimal music learning should imitate language learning: as students learn to speak and then to read language, students should learn to play and then to read music. The notation in the book is provided as a resource when a reminder is needed during the aural learning process. This volume should not be used as a "note by note" visual study guide for students when they are first learning the pieces.

About This Book

This volume is intended to be a resource of sequential material for use in a string class or other group ensemble situation and can also be used in a private lesson situation. The format, layout and materials of this book have been carefully chosen to reflect current unison teaching methodology.

This book includes the following:

1. A melody in standard music notation
   The melodies are traditional folk melodies in unison for all instruments. They are sequentially arranged to introduce and reinforce new technique or musical concepts.

2. A simple bass line in standard music notation
   The bass lines were written for all instruments as a means of introducing harmonic change. Bass lines can be used to teach basic bowing patterns, open string note reading and ear training in simple harmonic movement.

3. A simple harmony part in standard notation
   The harmony parts are rhythmically identical and technically similar to the melodies so that they can be learned immediately after mastering the melody. They require no additional technique except an occasional string crossing.

4. A melodic contour tablature with imbedded letter names for some repertoire
   The melodic contoured note tablature provides a visual reference for the contour of the melody and for the names of the notes. It can serve as a pre-reading tool to introduce and reinforce the musical alphabet, the geography of the fingerboard, visual tracking and pitch direction.

5. A "notes used in this piece" key to provide note name and finger numbers
   Standard fingerings are not written on the notes themselves in the student volume. The intent of not including fingerings in the student book is to allow each teacher to individualize the fingerings as they deem necessary.

The melody may be played and performed in a unison group or single instrument solo with piano accompaniment. The melody, harmony and bass line can be played together in traditional orchestral instrumentation or can be played by any combination of stringed instruments high to low including trios of like instruments. The piano part can be added or left out for practice or performance.

Reading Preparation

We believe that young students should develop posture, tone and intonation before beginning note reading and that older students will be most successful if playing and note reading are studied separately in the beginning stages. To that end we recommend using the notation as a reference guide while learning the melodic repertoire by ear. The notation can facilitate the study of note reading after the melodies are mastered. The bass lines and melody lines can be learned reading the notation at a later time.

Songs to Sing and Play by Ear

Chicken on a Fencepost

American Folk Song
Solo CD #2/A and 3/D   Piano CD #48/A   49/D   50/G   52/E

Chicken on a fencepost, Can't dance Josey. 3X Hello, Susan Brownie-o!

Old Brass Wagon

American Folk Song
Solo CD #4/A and 5/D   Piano CD #53/A   54/D   55/G   57/E

Circle to the left, now, Old brass wagon. 3X You're the one, my darling.

Hot Cross Buns should be learned by listening to the CD. Solo CD #6/A   7/D   Piano CD #58/A   59/D   60/G   62/E

Lucy Locket

English Folk Song
Solo CD #8/G   Piano CD #63/G

Lucy Locket lost her pocket. Kitty Fisher found it. Not a penny was there in it, only ribbon round it.

Teddy Bear should be learned by listening to the CD. Solo CD #9/G   Piano CD #64/G

Winter Has Come

German Folk Song
Solo CD #10   Ensemble #31   Piano CD #65

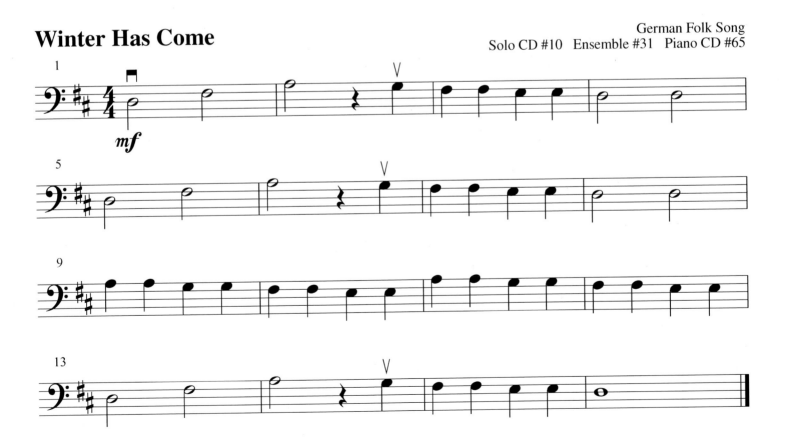

Twinkle, Twinkle Little Star

French/English Folk Song

Notes Used in This Piece

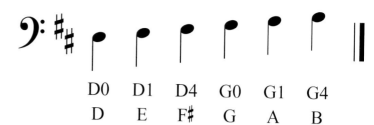

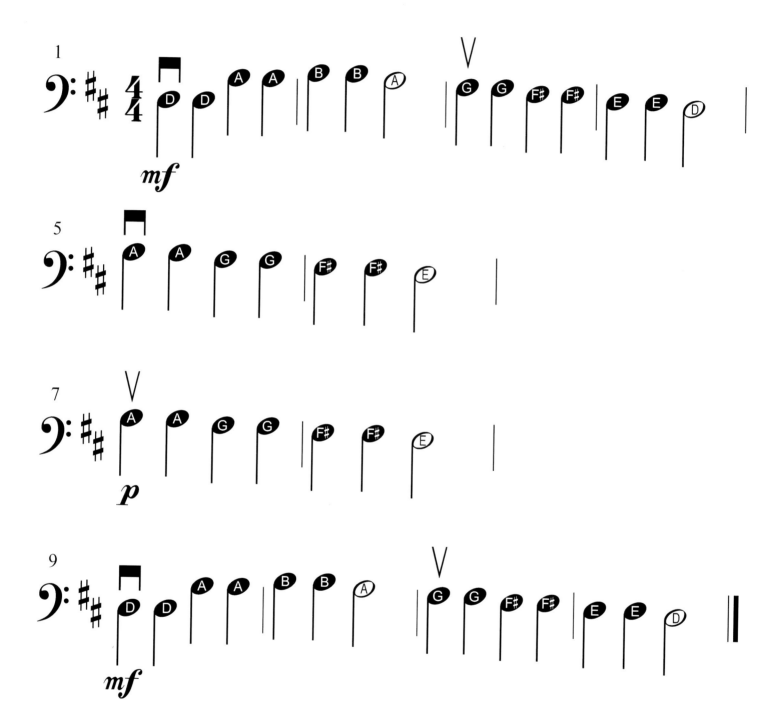

Twinkle, Twinkle Little Star

French/English Folk Song
Solo CD #11   Ensemble CD #32   Piano CD #66

Notes Used in This Piece

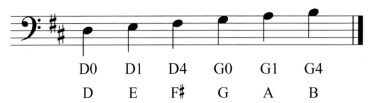

D0   D1   D4   G0   G1   G4
D   E   F♯   G   A   B

Melody

Bass Line

Harmony Part p. 29

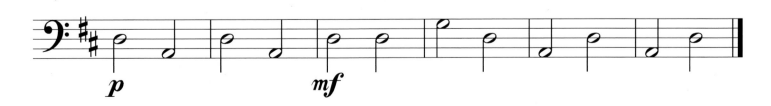

8

French Folk Song

French Folk Song

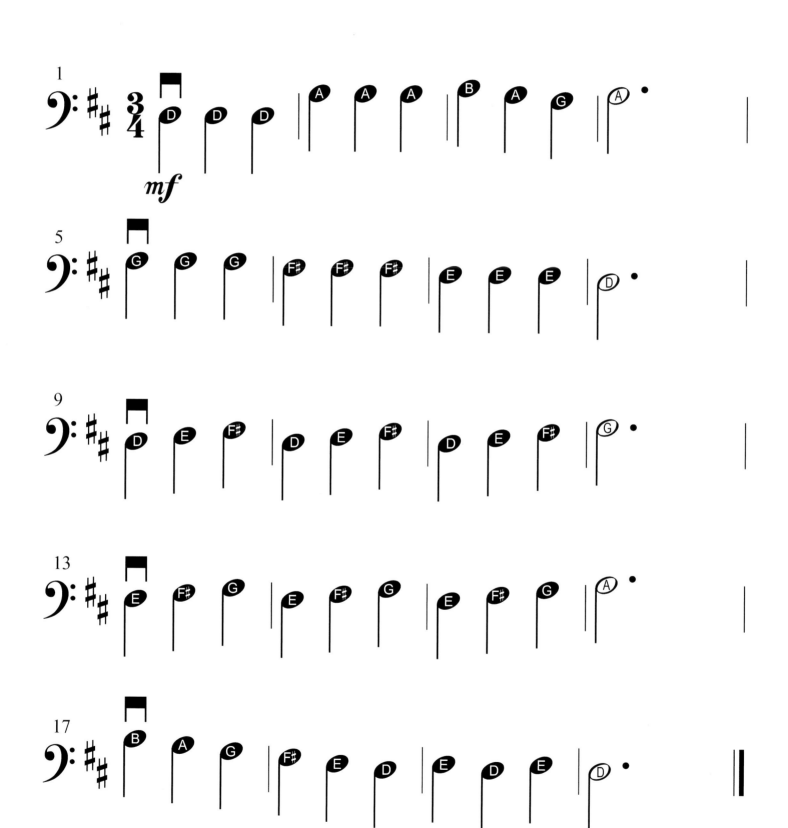

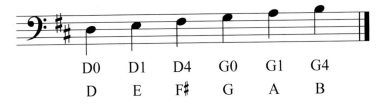

French Folk Song

French Folk Song
Solo CD #12   Ensemble CD #33   Piano CD #67

Notes Used in This Piece

D0	D1	D4	G0	G1	G4
D	E	F♯	G	A	B

Melody

Bass Line

Harmony Part p. 29

10

Lightly Row

German/English Folk Song

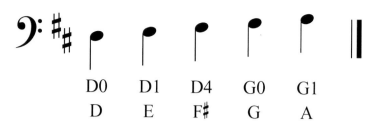

D0	D1	D4	G0	G1
D	E	F♯	G	A

Lightly Row

German/English Folk Song
Solo CD #13   Ensemble CD #34   Piano CD #68

Notes Used in This Piece

D0	D1	D4	G0	G1
D	E	F♯	G	A

Melody

Bass Line

Harmony Part p. 30

12

Rocky Mountain

American Folk Song

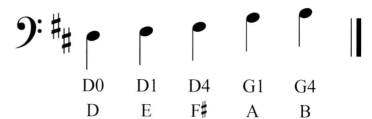

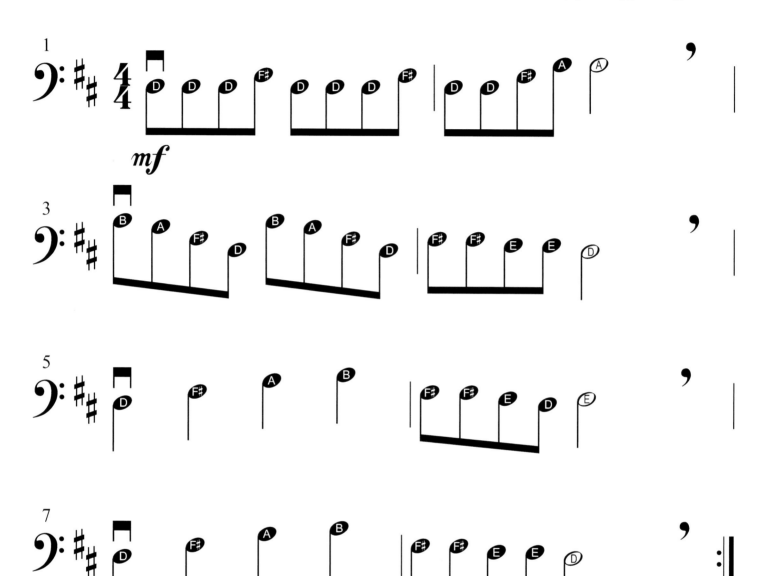

Rocky Mountain

American Folk Song
Solo CD #14 Ensemble CD #35 Piano CD #69

Notes Used in This Piece

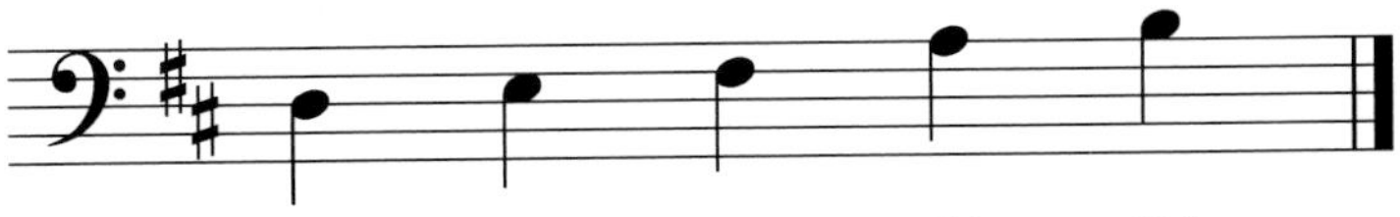

D0	D1	D4	G1	G4
D	E	F♯	A	B

Melody

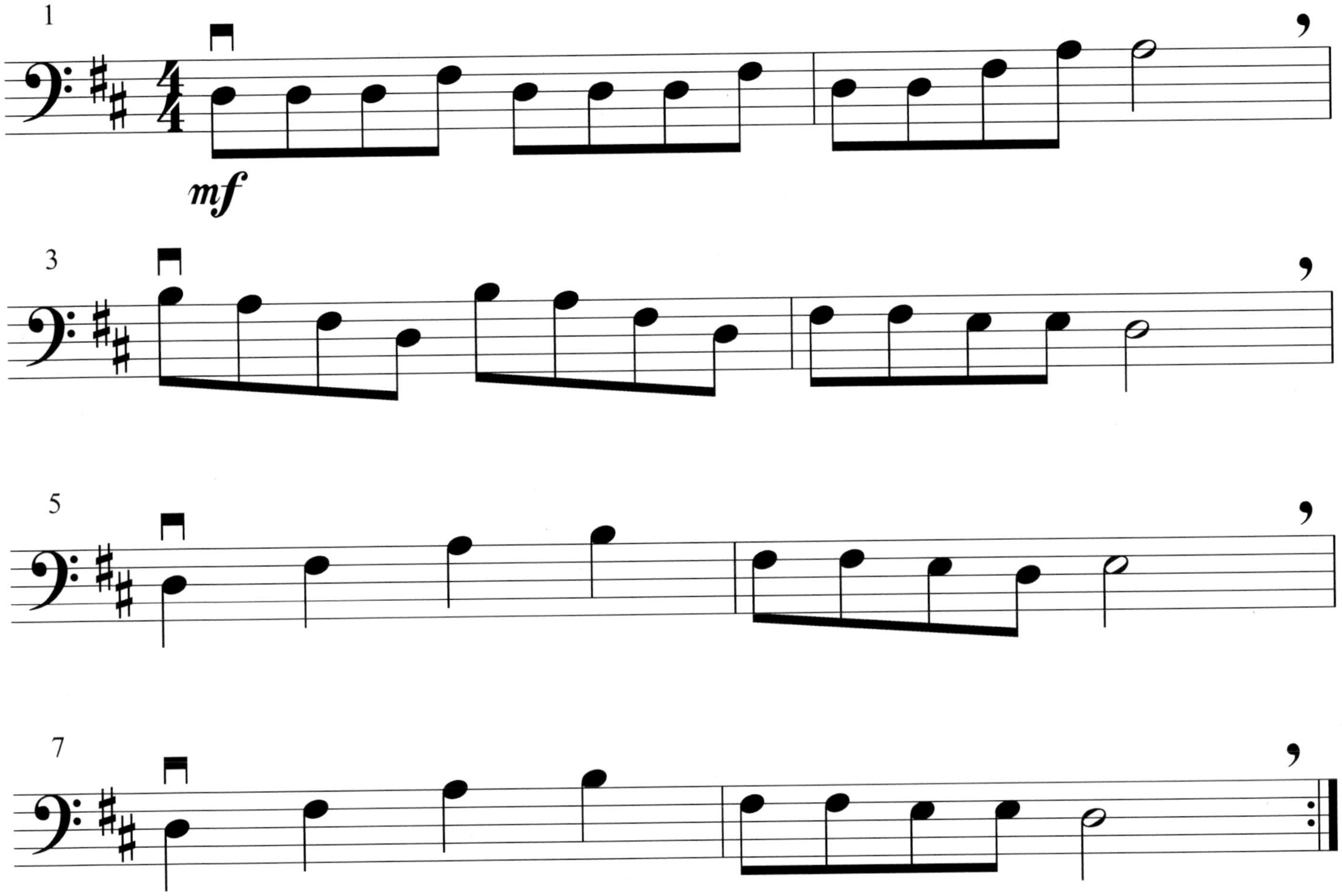

Bass Line

Harmony Part p. 30

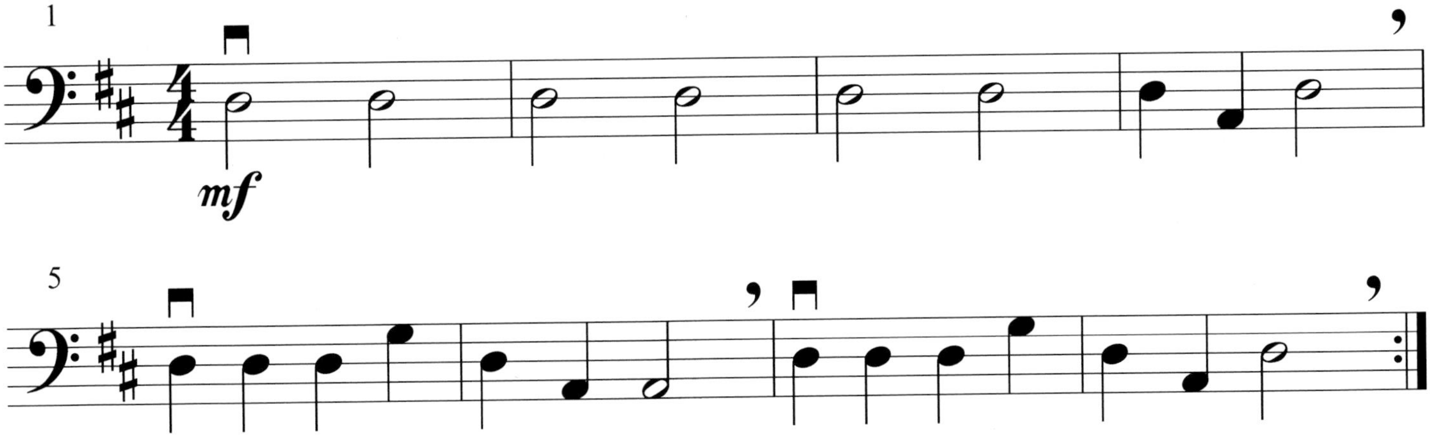

Lullaby

Jean-Jacques Rousseau

Notes Used in This Piece

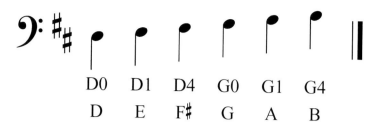

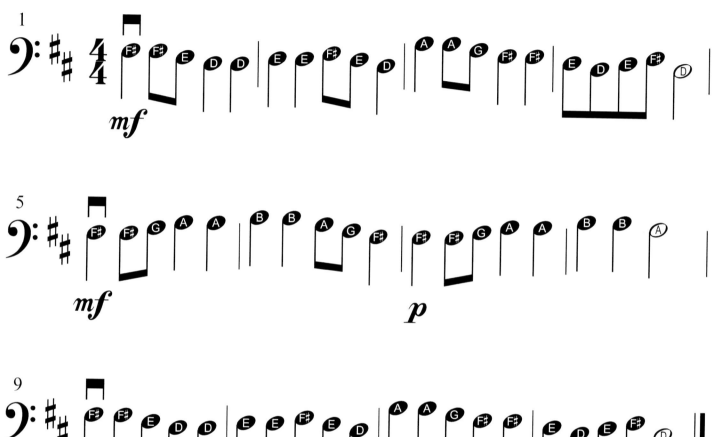

Lullaby

Jean-Jacques Rousseau
Solo CD #15   Ensemble CD #36   Piano CD #70

Notes Used in This Piece

Melody

Bass Line

Harmony Part p. 31

I Am a Fine Musician

German Folk Song

Notes Used in This Piece

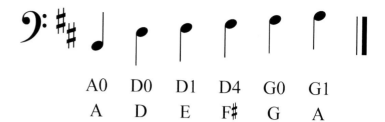

A0	D0	D1	D4	G0	G1
A	D	E	F♯	G	A

I Am a Fine Musician

German Folk Song
Solo CD #16   Ensemble CD #37   Piano CD #71

Notes Used in This Piece

A0 D0 D1 D4 G0 G1
A   D   E   F# G   A

Melody

5

9

13

Bass Line

Harmony Part p. 31

5

9

13

18

May Song

German Folk Song

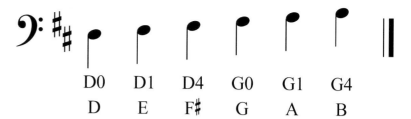

D0	D1	D4	G0	G1	G4
D	E	F#	G	A	B

May Song

German Folk Song
Solo CD #17   Ensemble CD #38   Piano CD #72

Notes Used in This Piece

D0	D1	D4	G0	G1	G4
D	E	F♯	G	A	B

Melody

Bass Line

Harmony Part p. 32

Martin's March

Winifred Crock
Solo CD #18   Ensemble CD #39   Piano CD #73

Notes Used in This Piece

| A0 | A1 | A4 | D0 | E0 |
| A | B | C♯ | D | E |

Melody

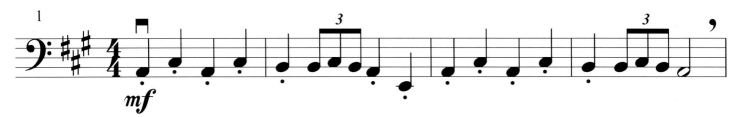

Bass Line   Harmony Part p. 32

Songs in 6/8 Meter

Oats, Peas, Beans

English Folk Song
Solo CD #19   Piano CD #74

Lazy Mary

English Folk Song
Solo CD #20   Piano CD #75

Pompey

English Folk Song
Solo CD #21   Piano CD #76

Weldon

American Folk Song
Solo CD #22   Ensemble CD #40   Piano CD #77

Notes Used in This Piece

D0	D1	D4	G0	G1	G4
D	E	F♯	G	A	B

Melody

Bass Line   Harmony Part p. 33

Weldon
Double Note Variation

American Folk Song
Solo CD #23   Ensemble CD #41   Piano CD #78

Notes Used in This Piece

D0	D1	D4	G0	G1	G4
D	E	F♯	G	A	B

Melody

This variation includes the preparation notes for the actual double bow variation.
When this variation is easy and comfortable try double bows on every note except the last half note.

 etc.

One Octave Scales

D Major Scale

D 1 4 G 1 4 III/2 III/4 III/4 III/2 I/4 1 G 4 1 D

G Major Scale

2 A 1 2 D 1 4 G G 4 1 D 2 1 A 2

C Major Scale

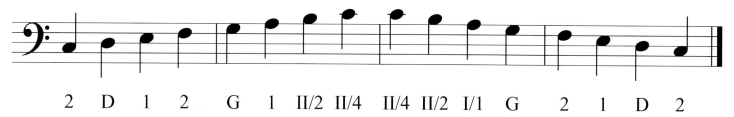

2 D 1 2 G 1 II/2 II/4 II/4 II/2 I/1 G 2 1 D 2

A Major Scale

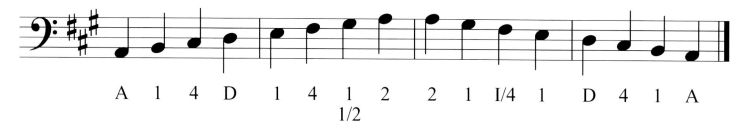

A 1 4 D 1 4 1 2 2 1 I/4 1 D 4 1 A
1/2

Bohemian Folk Song

Bohemian Folk Song
Solo CD #24   Ensemble CD #42   Piano CD #79

Notes Used in This Piece

Melody

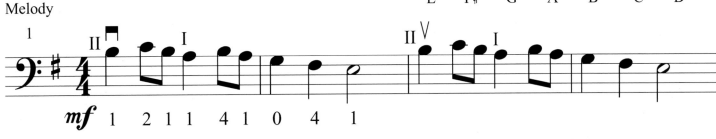

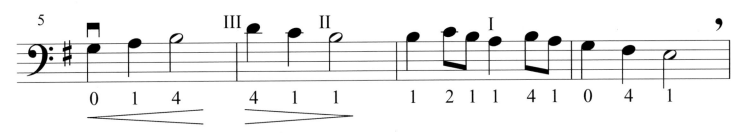

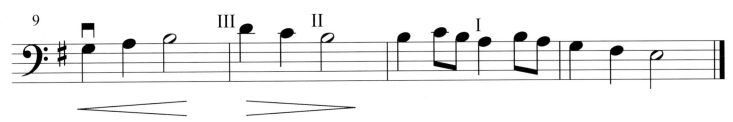

Bass Line

Harmony Part p. 33

Rigadoon

Henry Purcell
Solo CD #25   Ensemble CD #43   Piano CD #80

Notes Used in This Piece

D0	D1	D4	G0	G1	G4
D	E	F#	G	A	B

Allegro

Rigadoon
Bass Line

Harmony Part p. 34

Canons for Everyone

Canon in Two Voices

Tallis
Ensemble CD #44

Canon in Four Voices

Tallis
Ensemble CD #45

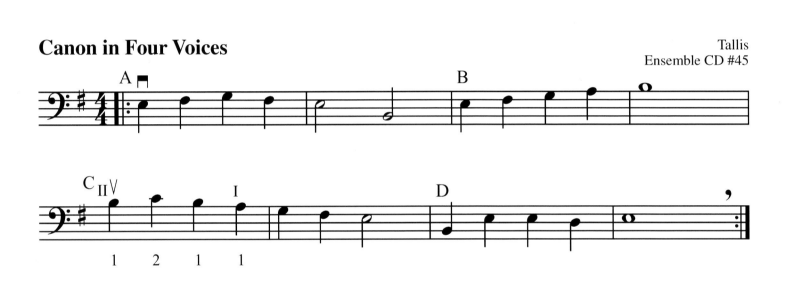

Canon in Three Voices

Folk Song
Ensemble CD #46

Twinkle, Twinkle Little Star
Harmony Part

French Folk Song
Harmony Part

Lightly Row
Harmony Part

Rocky Mountain
Harmony Part

Lullaby
Harmony Part

I Am a Fine Musician
Harmony Part

May Song
Harmony Part

Martin's March
Harmony Part

Weldon
Harmony Part

Bohemian Folk Song
Harmony Part

Rigadoon
Harmony Part

Chicken on a Fencepost
(Advanced Part)

Solo CD #26/A and #27/D
Piano CD #48/A 49/D 50/G 51/C

Old Brass Wagon
(Advanced Part)

Solo CD #28/A and #29/D
Piano CD #53/A 54/D 55/G 56/C